D1063763

MANNERS ON THE PLAYGROUND

by Emma Bassier

Cody Koala

An Imprint of Pop!
popbooksonline.com

abdobooks.com

Published by Pop!, a division of ABDO, PO Box 398166, Minneapolis, Minnesota 55439. Copyright © 2020 by POP, LLC. International copyrights reserved in all countries. No part of this book may be reproduced in any form without written permission from the publisher. Pop!™ is a trademark and logo of POP, LLC.

Printed in the United States of America, North Mankato, Minnesota

102019
012020

THIS BOOK CONTAINS RECYCLED MATERIALS

Cover Photo: iStockphoto
Interior Photos: iStockphoto, 1, 5, 7, 9 (top), 9 (bottom left), 9 (bottom right), 10, 13 (top), 13 (bottom left), 13 (bottom right), 14, 19, 21 (top left), 21 (top right), 21 (bottom); Shutterstock Images, 16–17

Editor: Brienna Rossiter
Series Designer: Jake Slavik

Library of Congress Control Number: 2019942769

Publisher's Cataloging-in-Publication Data

Names: Bassier, Emma, author.
Title: Manners on the playground / by Emma Bassier
Description: Minneapolis, Minnesota : Pop!, 2020 | Series: Manners matter | Includes online resources and index.
Identifiers: ISBN 9781532165641 (lib. bdg.) | ISBN 9781644942970 (pbk.) | ISBN 9781532166969 (ebook)
Subjects: LCSH: Manners--Juvenile literature. | Polite behavior--Juvenile literature. | Playgrounds--Juvenile literature. | Social customs--Juvenile literature.
Classification: DDC 395.12--dc23

Hello! My name is
Cody Koala

Pop open this book and you'll find QR codes like this one, loaded with information, so you can learn even more!

Scan this code* and others like it while you read, or visit the website below to make this book pop.

popbooksonline.com/manners-on-the-playground

*Scanning QR codes requires a web-enabled smart device with a QR code reader app and a camera.

Table of Contents

Chapter 1

Sharing Space

A boy digs in the sandbox. After a few minutes, he hands the shovel to his friend. The boy showed good **manners** by taking turns.

Watch a video here!

The playground is a common space. It does not belong to one person. Instead, many people go there to play. Manners help everyone have fun and feel **included**.

Chapter 2

Taking Turns

A playground has many fun things to do. People enjoy swings, slides, monkey bars, and more. **Polite** people take turns using the equipment.

Learn more here!

For example, suppose you want to go down a slide. To be polite, stand in line. Don't cut in front of others. Instead, be **patient**. Wait your turn. To use the slide again, go back to the end of the line.

A playground in Japan has a set of monkey bars with 556 **rungs**.

Chapter 3

Sharing Toys

People play with balls, shovels, and other toys at the playground. **Polite** people share these toys. That way, everyone gets a chance to use them.

Learn more here!

If you want a toy, don't grab it out of someone's hands. Instead, ask if you can use it. Also, make sure to give it back when you're done.

Remember that other people want to choose games and toys too.

Words help people show
good **manners**. For example,
if you want to use a toy or
join a game, say *please*.

Adding this word is a polite way to ask a question. If someone does what you ask, say *thank you*.

Chapter 4

Playing Games

People use **manners** when they play games. In tag, one person is "it." Some people always want to be "it." Other people never want to be "it." But **polite** people take turns.

Complete an activity here!

Some games have teams. It's okay to feel sad if your team loses. But it's not okay to push or hit. If your team wins, remember not to **brag**. Bragging can hurt people's feelings.

Take turns.

Share toys.

Say *please* and *thank you.*

Making Connections

Text-to-Self

What is your favorite thing to do on a playground?

Text-to-Text

Have you read other books about manners? How were those manners similar to or different from the manners described in this book?

Text-to-World

Some playgrounds are part of schools. Where else might you find a playground?

Glossary

brag – to talk proudly about winning or make someone feel bad for losing.

included – part of a group or game.

manners – the correct words or actions for certain situations.

patient – when someone waits for his or her turn without complaining.

polite – showing good manners.

rung – a horizontal bar, such as on a ladder.

Index

Online Resources

popbooksonline.com

Thanks for reading this Cody Koala book!

Scan this code* and others like it in this book, or visit the website below to make this book pop!

popbooksonline.com/manners-on-the-playground

*Scanning QR codes requires a web-enabled smart device with a QR code reader app and a camera.